Life in a
ROTTEN LOG

Malcolm Penny

Chicago, Illinois

© 2004 Raintree
Published by Raintree, a division of Reed Elsevier, Inc.
Chicago, Illinois
Customer Service 888-363-4266
Visit our website at www.raintreelibrary.com

All rights reserved. No part of this publication may be reproduced or utilized in any form or by any means, electronic or mechanical, including photocopying, recording, or by any information storage and retrieval system, without permission in writing from the publishers.

For information, address the publisher:
Raintree, 100 N. LaSalle, Suite 1200, Chicago, IL 60602

Project Editors: Marta Segal Block, Jennifer Mattson, Tamsin Osler
Production Manager: Brian Suderski
Designed by Ian Winton
Illustrated by Jim Chanell and Stuart Lafford

Planned and produced by Discovery Books

Library of Congress Cataloging-in-Publication Data:
Penny, Malcolm.
Life in a rotten log / Malcolm Penny.
v. cm. -- (Microhabitats)
Includes bibliographical references (p.) and index.
Contents: Falling branches, falling trees -- First arrivals -- Termites open the door -- Hunters and hunted -- Logs in water -- Threats.
ISBN 0-7398-6804-7 (Library Binding-hardcover) -- ISBN 1-4109-0349-4 (Paperback)
1. Forest ecology--Juvenile literature. [1. Forest ecology. 2. Forests and forestry. 3. Ecology.] I. Title. II. Series.
QH541.5.F6P447 2003
577.3--dc21
2003002659

Printed and bound in the United States
08 07 06 05 04
10 9 8 7 6 5 4 3 2 1

Acknowledgments
The publishers would like to thank the following for permission to reproduce photographs:
Front cover: Oxford Scientific Films; p.6: P. Clement/Bruce Coleman Collection; p.7: Dr. Eckhart Pott/Bruce Coleman Collection; p.8: M.Moffett (Minden Pictures)/Frank Lane Picture Agency; p.9: Derek Middleton/Frank Lane Picture Agency; p.10t: Stephen Krasemann/Natural History Photographic Agency; p.10m: PhotoDisc inc.; p.10b: PhotoDisc inc.; p.11: Barrie Watts/Oxford Scientific Films; p.13: Brian Rogers/Natural Visions; p.14: Dr. Rod Preston-Mafham/Premaphotos Wildlife; p.17: Jane Burton/Bruce Coleman Collection; p.18: G. Ellis/Frank Lane Picture Agency; p.20: Hans Reinhard/Bruce Coleman Collection; p. 21; L.West/Frank Lane Photographic Agency; p.22: Tony Tilford/Oxford Scientific Films; p.23: Ken Preston-Mafham/Premaphotos Wildlife; p.24: Daniel Cox/Oxford Scientific Films; p.25: Tero Niemi/Bruce Coleman Collection; p.26: Malcolm Penny/Oxford Scientific Films; p.28: Harold Taylor/Oxford Scientific Films; p.29: Alastair Shay/Oxford Scientific Films.

Some words are shown in bold, **like this.** You can find out what they mean by looking in the glossary.

Contents

Falling Trees   4
First Arrivals   6
Termite Time   12
Hunters and Hunted   20
Logs in Water   24
The Forest's Future   26
Protecting Log Life   28
Glossary   30
Further Reading   31
Index   32

Falling Trees

A New Beginning

It is never silent in the forest. When summer thunderstorms roar, or winter winds tear through the trees, it can be a scary place. Every once in a while you hear the creaking and groaning sounds of a falling tree. This is the end of a life that may be more than 200 years old—but it is the beginning of a new cycle of life, in and around the fallen log.

A Place to Live

At first the log provides small forest creatures with shelter from wind and rain. As it slowly rots away, animals and plants can get inside it. Some animals just visit the log, but others find it a perfect place for living and raising young. As the log gets older, more and more different forms of life make their homes there, while earlier residents leave as the wood becomes too soft for them.

Guess What?

- A tiny scratch made by a black bear in a tree trunk may let in **burrowing** beetles. They carry a **fungus** that can cause the death of a huge tree.

- A tree that lived for 200 years might take 300 or even 400 years to rot away completely on a forest floor.

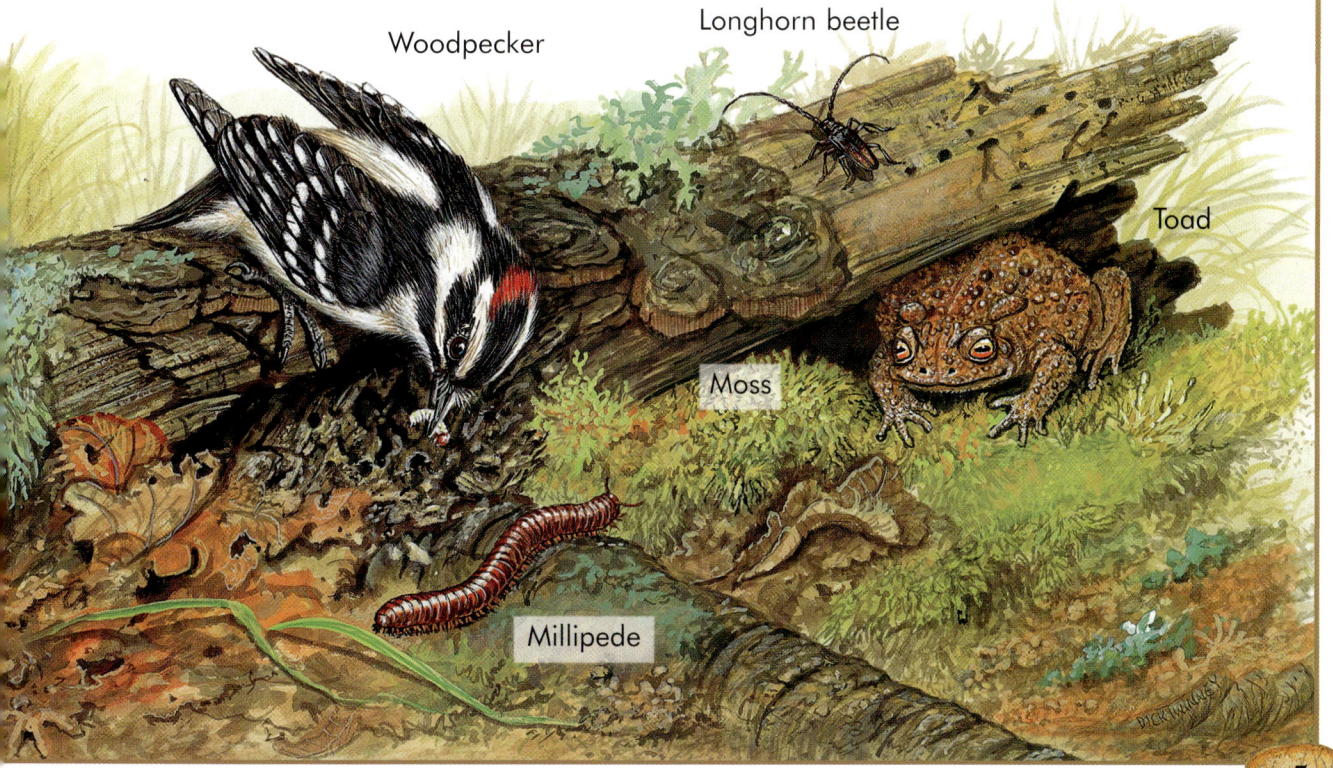

Woodpecker · Longhorn beetle · Toad · Moss · Millipede

First Arrivals

A Newly Fallen Log

Small **mammals** such as mice and voles take shelter under a newly fallen log. The best shelter is from a log that has fallen across a slope, because it is easier to crawl underneath where the ground falls away on the downhill side. The animals can hide from **predators** under this natural roof during the day.

A bank vole needs to find shelter from bad weather and a safe place to hide.

Bark beetle larvae make tunnels leading from the place where the mother lays her eggs.

Invaders

The first animals to invade the log are bark beetles that break into its tough surface. The female beetles lay their eggs underneath the bark. The wormlike babies, called **larvae,** hatch out of the eggs. They chew their way through the wood, causing the bark to loosen. Other kinds of beetles soon move in—followed by the animals that hunt them.

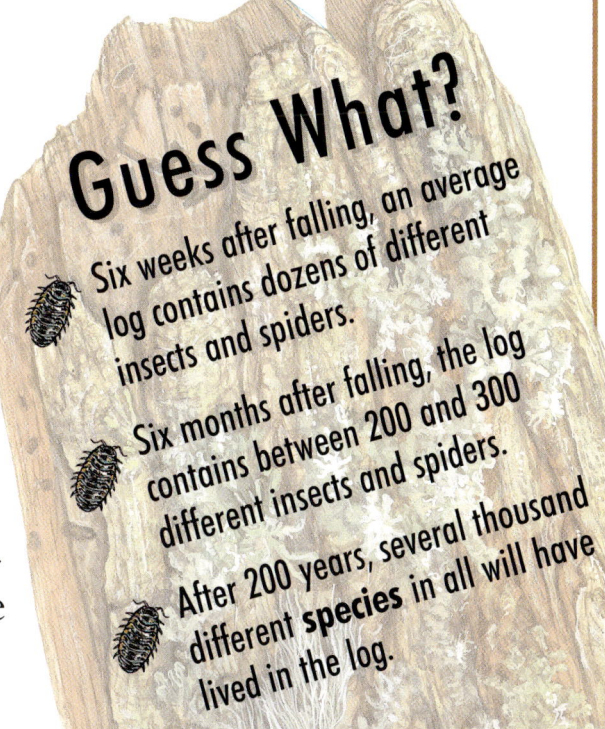

Guess What?

- Six weeks after falling, an average log contains dozens of different insects and spiders.
- Six months after falling, the log contains between 200 and 300 different insects and spiders.
- After 200 years, several thousand different **species** in all will have lived in the log.

Fungus Farmers

As it rots, the sweet inner bark of the log produces a smell that attracts ambrosia beetles. They arrive by the hundreds, and the females dig tunnels under the bark. As they do so, they release a scent that attracts male ambrosia beetles to mate with them. Then the female beetles lay eggs in the log.

An ambrosia beetle larva (right) will develop into a **pupa** (center). The adult (left) will dig its way into the open air.

Ambrosia beetles act like farmers. They **burrow** into the dead wood, making small rooms. The beetles carry tiny **fungus** seeds, or **spores,** into the rooms, where the spores soon begin to grow. Later the beetles return to eat the fungus.

Deep Borers

Larger beetles such as the stag beetle lay eggs in a log when it has been rotting for awhile and is much softer. The **larvae** burrow deeper into the log when they hatch. A stag beetle larva remains inside the log for three to six years, feeding only on wood until it is fully grown. When it is ready to turn into an adult, the larva is about 5 inches (13 centimeters) long.

A stag bettle explores a fallen log.

Guess What?

- The biggest beetle in the world is the goliath beetle from West Africa. It breeds in dead wood, weighs 2.5–3.5 oz (70–100 g), and is nearly 5 in. (13 cm) long.
- The longhorn beetle does not only attack dead trees—it is also a serious pest to living trees, causing damage as it chews through the wood.

Wet Wood

The **burrows** made by the beetles let water into the log. Other animals crowd into the damp wood, along with **fungi**. Some of these fungi cause the log to rot.

Wax-gill or neon mushrooms

Bracket fungi

Fungi can grow in the dark. Instead of changing sunlight into food like plants, fungi get their energy by breaking down the **cells** of damp wood or any kind of dead matter. This releases the **nutrients** in the cells, which the fungi then absorb. By rotting the log in this way, fungi return important nutrients back to the forest soil.

These fruit bodies are ready to release their spores.

Fruit Bodies

A fungus spreads through the wood in a network of thin threads. When it is big enough, the fungus produces **fruit bodies,** like toadstools or mushrooms. The fruit bodies release **spores** that carry the fungus to other dead logs.

A puffball mushroom sends its spores into the air.

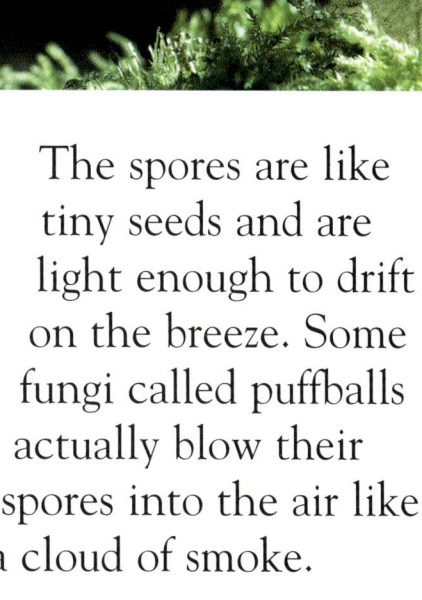

Guess What?

A tree fungus known as the fuzzy sandozi has a fruit body that grows to 55 in. (140 cm) across, and can weigh 300 lb (135 kg). It is the largest fungus in the United States, and probably in the world. Only four or five have ever been found, all in the states of Oregon and Washington.

Large, flat fruit bodies that grow on rotten logs, called bracket fungi, are often full of tiny rove beetles that feed on the fungus.

The spores are like tiny seeds and are light enough to drift on the breeze. Some fungi called puffballs actually blow their spores into the air like a cloud of smoke.

Termite Time

Enter the Termites

When the dead log has been rotting on the forest floor for nine or ten years, new invaders arrive. The **fungi** have prepared the way for termites to get in. A large termite colony can contain tens of thousands of workers, all controlled by a single queen.

Deep inside the termite nest, the queen (the large, fat termite in the middle) lays eggs that the workers will carry away to raise in special chambers when they hatch.

Wood Eaters

Termites eat wood, but they cannot digest it. Instead, they have tiny **microorganisms** living in their **guts** that break down **cellulose**, the tough substance that makes up plant cells. These microorganisms convert the cellulose into simpler substances that the termites can then digest and absorb into their bodies.

Armies of termite workers go out to collect food for the young in their nest.

See for Yourself

Find a log or a piece of wood that has been lying for a few years in a damp place (at the edge of a sports field or behind a shed would be good places to look). Turn it over and you might find **burrows** underneath. Can you guess some of the animals that have made them?

Carpenter Ants

The rotten log may also contain a nest of large, black carpenter ants. They hollow out chambers in the wood to live in, but unlike termites, they do not eat the wood. Instead, they look for food at night and bring whatever they find back to the nest for their queen and the young ants.

Carpenter ants in Borneo drag a dead wasp to their nest.

Their main food is honeydew, a liquid produced by small plant bugs called aphids. Carpenter ants carry honeydew back to the nest in their stomachs, where they **regurgitate** the honeydew, or bring it back up from their stomachs, to feed to the other ants. They also gather dead insects, and sometimes raid houses for sugar and scraps of meat.

Teamwork

Every nest contains three different types of carpenter ant: a queen who lays all the eggs, and two kinds of worker ants, major workers and minor workers. The major workers guard the nest and search for food, while the smaller minor workers help expand the nest and care for the young.

Here is a carpenter ant queen (top), a major worker (middle), and a minor worker (bottom).

See for Yourself

The nests of common black ants are not hard to find on any piece of dry ground, because the ants leave a ring of loose dirt around the entrance to the nest.

If you find a nest, watch the entrance without touching the ants. You will see workers coming and going. What are they taking out, and what are they bringing in?

Salamanders

Salamanders are **amphibians,** or animals that spend part of their lives on land and part in water. They need a cool, damp place to live, especially during dry summers. A rotten log is perfect for them.

Slimy salamander

Red salamander

Salamanders feed on worms, snails, and insects, mainly at night—and they may also eat each other.

To defend themselves against **predators,** salamanders produce an awful-smelling substance, which may be poisonous to any animal that bites them.

Spotted salamander

Eggs and Babies

The female salamander of some **species** may lay eggs inside the log, or sometimes out on the damp forest floor. The **larvae** of these salamanders pass through a tadpole stage inside the eggs. They already have lungs when they hatch. Other species of salamander lay eggs in water like frogs. The eggs hatch into tadpoles with **gills,** and later the tadpoles develop legs and move onto land to live.

Guess What?

The tails of some salamanders drop off if the salamander is attacked. The tail then twitches on the ground and distracts the attacker while the salamander escapes. Many lizards have tails that can do the same thing.

A type of salamander called a mudpuppy never takes an an adult form. It still looks like a tadpole even when it is old enough to breed.

A newly hatched fire salamander larva breathes underwater with feathery gills on each side of its head.

Deer Mice

When the log has been hollowed out by beetles, termites, and **fungi**, it can become a home for small **mammals**. One of them, the deer mouse, plays a part in helping the forest to grow.

Truffle Eaters

Truffles grow in woodlands and forests all around the world. They are fungi that grow under the forest floor and have a delicious smell. Deer mice love to eat truffles more than anything, even though they also eat seeds and insects. The mice sniff out the truffles and dig them up.

A deer mouse timidly explores the forest floor.

Spreading Spores

When a mouse has eaten them, the truffle **spores** pass out in the mouse's droppings. This spreads the fungus around the forest. The spores produce many tiny threads, which wrap themselves around the roots of the trees.

The truffle fungus takes a little sugar from the tree roots, but in return the tree receives **nutrients** that the fungus collects from the soil.
The tree cannot collect enough of these nutrients for itself, though they are important for it to grow properly. In this way the fungus helps the forest grow.

Guess What?

The California red-backed vole weighs only about 1 oz (28 g). It **burrows** underneath rotting logs and feeds only on truffles, spreading their spores throughout the soil.

Trees planted in new areas where there are no truffles in the soil do not grow as well as trees in older forests.

Deer mice and a squirrel hunt for truffles under the forest floor.

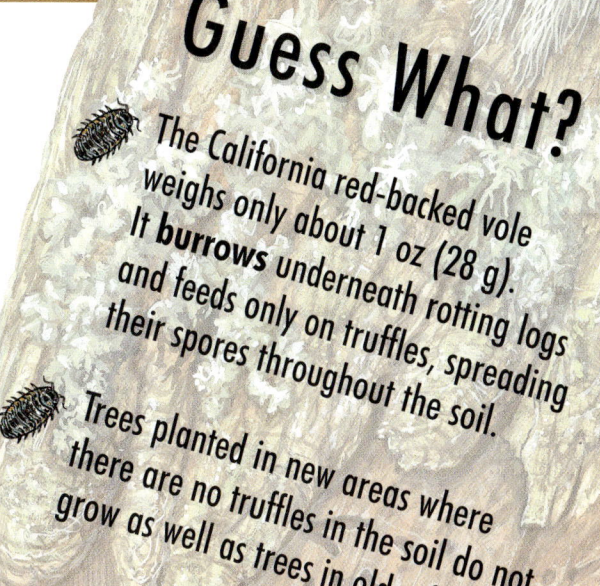

Hunters and Hunted

Scavengers

The rotting log is a busy hunting ground for an enormous number of small animals. Millipedes are important because they crunch through wood. Pill bugs (also known as wood lice or roly-polies) eat some of the crunched-up bits of wood the millipedes leave behind, and springtails eat even smaller pieces. These are all **scavengers**—animals that eat scraps and leftovers. Under the log there are also many animals that are **predators**. These predators include hunting beetles, centipedes, and spiders.

Pill bugs have a tough outer shell like a suit of armor, but they also produce chemicals to protect themselves from predators.

Poison Defenses

To defend themselves, millipedes produce chemicals that are poisonous. One of its predators has found a way around this defense. It is called a ground beetle, or carabid. With its extremely long jaws, it can keep its head at a safe distance from its **prey** when it bites.

Most millipedes are black or brown, but this Californian millipede is more brightly colored to scare predators.

Guess What?

- The difference between millipedes and centipedes is that millipedes have two pairs of legs per segment, while centipedes have only one pair per segment.
- The longest millipede in the world lives in Seychelles, a group of islands off the eastern coast of Africa. It is over 11 in. (28 cm) long and 0.75 in. (2 cm) wide.
- The millipede with the most legs—355 pairs—lives in South Africa. The centipede with the most legs—177 pairs—can be found in southern Europe.

Pill bugs under attack produce a terrible-smelling chemical to turn away predators. The pill bug's main enemy is a spider called *Dysdera* that has very long jaws.

Wood Wasps

Wood wasps are large insects only distantly related to true wasps. They have no sting although the female has a long spike at the back of her body used for laying eggs. The female selects a weak or dying trunk or branch, pushes her spike deep into the wood, and then lays her eggs.

A female wood wasp (above) lays her egg deep inside a branch. Her larva (right) will use its sharp jaws to chew its way out of the wood when it hatches.

The **larvae** hatch from the eggs as **grubs,** and tunnel through the wood for nearly a year before turning into **pupae** and then into adult wood wasps.

Enemies of Wood Wasps

Even deep inside a log, the wood wasp grubs are not completely safe. They may be dug out by woodpeckers, which like to eat the grubs, or they may be attacked by insects called ichneumon flies.

First the female ichneumon fly senses a wood wasp grub with her **antennae**. She then drills into the wood with her spike, stings the grub, and lays an egg on its back. The sting **paralyzes** the insect (makes it unable to move), and when the egg hatches, the ichneumon grub gradually eats the wood wasp grub.

Guess What?

- Before she lays eggs, a wood wasp injects a liquid containing particles of **fungus** under the bark. The larva will need the fungus to help it grow, but the fungus may also kill the tree.
- One wood wasp can lay 25 eggs in a single branch before going to another branch to lay more.
- Wood wasps often lay eggs in dead branches while the rest of the tree is still alive.

A female ichneumon fly probes deep to lay an egg on a wood wasp grub that she has found.

Logs in Water

Bridges and Shelters

Trees that fall across streams help the forest animals by providing bridges for them. Those that fall into streams are even more important. Logs in streams provide shelter for all kinds of animals, especially in the winter rains. Fallen logs also slow the current down so that it drops the **sediment**—particles of dirt or sand—that the water carries, instead of washing it further down the stream.

This sediment lands on the bottom of the stream, where it provides homes for **burrowing** creatures and a place where plants can grow. A muddy stream bed is full of life.

A fallen log makes it easier for this black bear to cross the river.

Kingfishers come to feed where fallen logs shelter small fish.

Homes for Fish

Logs in streams are good breeding places for fish and shelter for their food, such as water plants and young caddisflies and dragonflies. They are also important feeding places for birds, which eat insects and small fish.

Guess What?

- Forestry workers used to think that logs in streams should be cleared away because they got in the way of the water flow, but now we know that it is better not to move them.

- Logs under water decay much more slowly than those on land, because there is not as much oxygen under water. Oxygen speeds up decay.

The Forest's Future

A Good Beginning

In the poor and heavily shaded soil of the forest floor, smothered by ferns and other plants, new seedlings may find it hard to grow. But seeds that fall on a rotting log, raised above the ground and spongy with damp mosses and **fungi**, are off to a good start.

Lined up in a row, these trees grew up along a nurse log.

Growth along a nurse log

1. Seedlings grow on the damp nurse log.

2. The log provides water and food for their roots.

Nurse Logs

Trees in old forests often grow in straight lines, looking as if they were planted by people. They have curved roots holding them above the ground. This shows that they grew along rotting logs, known as **nurse logs.**

As they grow up, their roots reach around the nurse log to the ground. This is why they are curved. The nurse log finally rots away, leaving the trees standing along the straight line where the log once was.

Guess What?

- The floor of an old forest may contain as much as 265 tons (240 metric tons) of rotting wood per acre (0.5 hectares).
- Rotting logs help the forest to grow, because they slowly release **nutrients** into the soil.
- A major threat to life in ancient forests is loggers who remove fallen logs to make their work easier.

3. The young trees stretch their roots around the log.

4. The nurse log rots, leaving the new trees standing in a straight line.

Protecting Log Life

Your Backyard

Even a woodpile in a suburban or city backyard is an important **microhabitat**. Logs cut in one fall will need to be left to dry for at least a year, and a lot can happen in that time.

A woodpile is full of nooks and crannies where animals can take shelter.

People who have a woodpile need to be careful when they take logs off the pile for the fire. All kinds of animals may be living there, including spiders, millipedes, pill bugs, and springtails. The woodpile may also attract animals such as toads and salamanders that need to **hibernate**, or sleep through the winter. Anyone removing a log should give the animals a chance to escape and try to leave any hibernating creatures a safe place to hide.

Wolf spider

Springtail

In the Woods

Around towns and cities there are always small patches of woodland, often thought of as worthless. But for very small creatures, they are not worthless at all. A rotten log in one of these areas supports just the same variety of life as a log in a much larger forest. No matter how large or small, all woodlands are worth protecting.

Guess What?

- In northern states, some frogs and newts spend more time asleep than awake: they hibernate for as long as eight months.
- Furniture beetle **larvae**, known as woodworms, do not need logs that are damp. They can develop from egg to adult without a drop of water.
- Bracket **fungi** that grow on dead wood are too tough for people to eat, but are a valuable source of food for mice and many insects.

A rotten log makes a perfect home for many kinds of fungi.

Glossary

amphibian animal that spends part of its life on land and part of its life in water

antenna (more than one are antennae) feeler on an insect's head that picks up smells and feels objects

burrow to dig a hole or tunnel in the ground. A hole or tunnel used as an animal's home is called a burrow.

cell smallest unit making up the body of any plant or animal

cell wall structure that supports and protects a plant cell

cellulose tough substance that forms the cell walls in plant cells

fruit body structure produced by a fungus that allows the fungus to spread its spores (seeds)

fungus (more than one are fungi) organisms made up of tiny hairs that spread over matter, dissolve it, and then absorb it. Molds and mushrooms are types of fungi.

gill feathery body structure that allows fish and some other animals to breathe underwater

grub any insect larva that looks like a worm

gut long tube that runs through an animal's body, through which food moves and wastes leave; intestine

hibernate spend the winter in a special kind of deep sleep

larva (more than one are larvae) young insect during the early stages of its life, when it looks nothing like its parents

mammal warm-blooded animal, usually with fur or hair, that gives birth to live young and nourishes it on mother's milk

microhabitat particular small area, such as inside a rotten log or under a stone, where certain animals live and plants grow

microorganism form of life too small to see without a microscope

nurse log rotten log that provides a good place for young trees to start their lives

nutrients minerals and other substances in soil that nourish or feed a plant and help it to grow

organism any living thing

paralyze cause an animal to be unable to move

predator animal that hunts other animals for food

prey animal that is hunted by other animals for food

pupa (more than one are pupae) stage in an insect's life just before it changes from a larva into an adult

regurgitate bring food that has been swallowed back up from the stomach

scavenger animal that gathers and eats the remains of food left behind by other animals

sediment small particles in water, such as sand or dirt

species group of living things that share certain features and are able to breed together

spore type of seed with a hard outer coating, produced by a fungus

Further Reading

Green, Jen. *A Dead Log.* New York: Crabtree, 1999.

Kittinger, Jo S. *Dead Log Alive.* New York: Scholastic Library, 1996.

Oliver, Clare. *Microhabitats: Life in a Tree.* Chicago: Raintree, 2002.

Pfeffer, Wendy. *A Log's Life.* New York: Simon and Schuster, 1997.

Index

ambrosia beetles 8
amphibians 16
ants 14–15
aphids 14

bacteria 13
bark beetles 4, 7
bear 24
beetles 5, 7, 8-9, 11, 18, 20, 21, 29
birds 23, 25
black ants 15
black bears 5, 24
bracket fungi 4, 10, 11, 29
burrows 7, 8, 9, 10, 13, 19, 24

caddisflies 25
California red-backed voles 19
Californian millipedes 21
carabids (see ground beetles)
carpenter ants 14–15
cellulose 13
centipedes 20, 21

daddy longlegs 4
deer mice 18
dragonflies 25
Dysdera spiders 21

eggs 7, 12, 15, 17, 22, 23, 29

fire salamanders 17
fish 25
forests 18, 19, 26, 27
frogs 29
fruit bodies 10, 11
fungi 4, 8, 10–11, 12, 18, 19, 23, 26, 29

furniture beetles 29
fuzzy sandozi 11
goliath beetles 9
ground beetles 21

hibernating animals 28, 29
honeydew 14
hunting beetles 20

ichneumon flies 23
insects 7, 16, 18, 22, 23, 29

kingfishers 25

larvae 7, 8, 9, 17, 22, 23, 25, 29
lichen 4
lizards 17
logs in water 24–25
loggers 27
longhorn beetles 9

mammals 6, 18, 19
mice 6, 18, 19, 29
microorganisms 13
millipedes 5, 20, 21, 28
mosses 5, 26
mudpuppies 17
mushrooms 4, 10, 11

nests 13, 14, 15
newts 29
nurse logs 26–27
nutrients 10, 19

pill bugs 4, 20, 21, 28
predators 6, 16, 20
prey 21
puffballs 11
pupae 8, 22

regurgitation 14
rove beetles 11

salamanders 16–17, 28
scavengers 20
sediment 24
seedlings 26
snails 16
spiders 7, 20, 21, 28
spores 8, 10, 11, 19
springtails 20, 28
squirrels 19
stag beetles 9
streams 24-25

termites 4, 12–13, 18
threats 27
toads 5, 28
toadstools 11
trees 4, 5, 19, 23, 26–27
truffles 18–19

voles 4, 6, 19

water plants 25
wolf spiders 28
wood wasps 4, 22–23
wood lice (see pill bugs)
woodpeckers 5, 23
woodpiles 28
woodworms (see furniture beetles)
worms 16

Edison Twp. Pub. Library
340 Plainfield Ave.
Edison, NJ 08817

FEB 6 - 2004

Edison Twp. Pub. Library
340 Plainfield Ave.
Edison, NJ 08817

FEB 6 - 2004